Contents

Special Stories ... 4
Matthew 13; Mark 4; Luke 8

The Good Samaritan ... 8
Luke 10

The Rich Fool ... 11
Luke 12

Be Ready ... 12
Luke 12

The Wise and Foolish Girls ... 13
Matthew 25

The Great Banquet ... 15
Matthew 22; Luke 14

Lost and Found ... 18
Matthew 18; Luke 15

The Prodigal Son ... 20
Luke 15

The Rich Man and the Beggar ... 23
Luke 16

Bags of Gold ... 26
Matthew 25; Luke 19

The Last Will Be First ... 27
Matthew 20

The Wicked Tenants ... 30
Matthew 21; Mark 12; Luke 20

Special Stories

Many of the people who came to listen to Jesus were farmers, or grew their own food. Jesus tried to pass on his message in a way that they would understand. He made up stories, called parables, to let people think things through for themselves. To some they would just be stories, but others would understand the real message . . .

"A farmer went out to sow some seeds," said Jesus, looking at the eager faces all around him. "As he was scattering it, some fell along the path and were trampled on, eaten by birds. Some fell on rocky ground where there was no soil.

JESUS the STORY TELLER

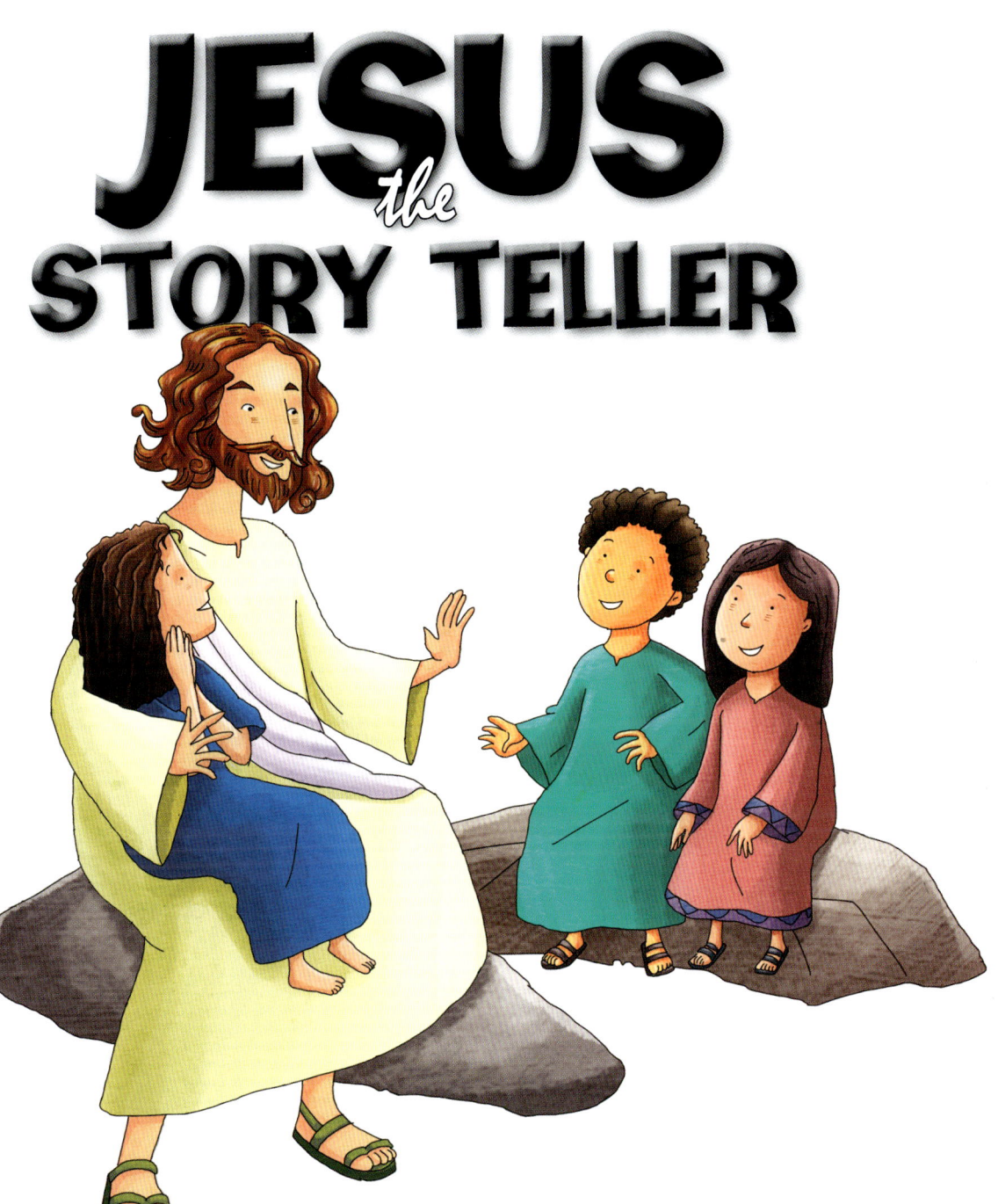

tales from the New Testament
retold for children

Jesus, the Story Teller
© 2023 North Parade Publishing,
Written by Janice Emmerson
Illustrations by QBS Learning

Published by North Parade Publishing, Bath BA1 1LF, United Kingdom

All rights are reserved. No part of this publication may be reproduced, stored in a retrieval system or transmitted in any form or by any means, electronic, mechanical, photocopying, recording or otherwise, without the prior permission of the Publisher

Printed in China

When those seeds began to grow, they withered and died quickly because their roots couldn't reach water. Other seeds fell among weeds which wrapped round them and choked them. But some seeds—a few—fell on good soil and grew into strong, healthy plants and produced a wonderful crop, far greater than what was sown."

Jesus was telling them he was like the farmer, and the seeds were like the message he brought from God. The seeds that fell on the path are like those people who hear the good news but pay no attention. Those that fell on the rocky ground are like people who are filled with joy when they first learn about the message, but have no roots, and so when life gets difficult they give up easily. The seeds among weeds are like those who hear but let themselves become overwhelmed and sidetracked by all of life's worries and pleasures.

But the seeds that fell on good soil are like those who hear God's message and hold it tight in their heart. Their faith grows and grows!

Jesus told another parable:

"Once a farmer spent a day sowing seed in his field, but that night, his enemy sowed weeds among the wheat. When the wheat began to grow, weeds grew too, mixed in with the good plants. His servants asked their master if they should pull the weeds up, but he replied, 'If you pull the weeds up, you may pull some of the wheat up too. We will have to let both grow until harvest, then we will collect and burn the weeds, and gather the wheat and bring it into my barn.'"

Later, the disciples asked Jesus what the story meant. He explained, "The farmer who sowed the good seed is the Son of Man. The field is the world, and the good seed is the people of the kingdom. The weeds were sown by the devil, and they are *his* people. The harvest will come at the end of time. Then the Son of Man will send out his angels. They will weed out of his kingdom

everything that causes sin and all those people who do evil things and think evil thoughts and throw them into the blazing furnace. But those people who are good will shine as brightly as the sun in the kingdom of their Father."

If you have a vegetable garden, however carefully you look after it, there are probably some nasty weeds too. If we try to dig them out, we might dig out some of the good plants. If we use weedkiller, most don't know the difference between one plant and the next and will just kill everything! So sometimes, it is best to wait until harvest time. Then you can pull up and enjoy all your wonderful fruit and vegetables and throw the weeds on the bonfire!

The Good Samaritan

When God gave Moses the special commandments so long ago, there were two commandments more important than all the rest—"Love God with all your heart, and all your soul," and "Love your neighbour just as you love yourself." These commandments are very important, because if people truly love God and truly love other people, they will want to follow all the other commandments anyway.

However, one time, someone asked Jesus, "But who exactly *is* my neighbour?" and Jesus told this story . . .

"Once there was a man who was travelling from Jerusalem to Jericho. He was walking along the dusty road when all of a sudden some men jumped out and began hitting and kicking him. They pushed him to the ground and stole everything he had with him—even his clothes. They left him in a ditch by the roadside and ran off.

"The poor man lay bleeding by the side of the road, barely able to lift his head. After a while, a priest came by. Now, the priest saw the beaten man, but he looked away and turned his horse towards the other side of the road, as far away from him as he could get. He carried on his way without one further glance.

"Time passed, and then another man came walking along the road. This man was a Levite who worked in the temple in Jerusalem. But he, too, turned his face the other way and quickly walked by without stopping.

"Then, along the road, came a Samaritan." (Jews and Samaritans didn't get on, so no one would have expected him to stop.) "He didn't see his enemy by the roadside—he saw a poor injured man who needed help. He knelt beside him, and carefully washed and bandaged his wounds. Then he helped him onto his donkey and took him to an inn. He even gave the innkeeper money to care for him."

Jesus looked at the man who had asked him the question. "So," he asked, "who do *you* think was a good neighbour to the injured man?"

The man sheepishly replied, "The one who was kind to him."

Jesus said, "Then go and be like him."

Being a good neighbour to someone isn't about where *they* live or where *you* live. It is about showing God's wonderful love to all those in need, whoever they are and wherever they may be.

The Rich Fool

Jesus wanted to warn his followers to be on their guard against all kinds of greed. Life shouldn't be about owning lots of things or making lots of money. He explained this to them in a parable:

"Once there was a very rich man. One year, he had such a big harvest that he didn't have enough room to store it. Instead of sharing it, he built huge new barns for his grain. Now he could take life easy!

"But God said to him, 'You fool, this very night your life will be over, and who will have all this then?'"

The rich man couldn't take his wealth with him after his death. His greed and selfishness would do him no good in the end. We shouldn't spend our lives laying up treasure for ourselves—we should use whatever God gives us to help others, and then we will be rich towards God.

Be Ready

Jesus told his followers they needed to be ready at all times for the day when he would come again. He told them a story about some good servants who were waiting for their master to return from a wedding feast. They didn't know when he would be back, for in those times wedding feasts could last for days! Nevertheless, the faithful servants stayed up, and kept the lamps cheerfully burning, so that the instant he knocked upon the door, they could open it for him.

Jesus went on to say that the servants would be richly rewarded for their readiness, for when he came back, the master be so pleased with them that he would put on an apron, sit them down at the table and wait on them himself! This is how Jesus will reward us if he returns to find us ready for him.

So let us be ready, for if we are not prepared when Jesus comes, there will be no time to get ready then. Let him instead find us watching, waiting and serving God as best we can.

The Wise and Foolish Girls

Jesus told his followers another story to help them to understand that they must be ready at all times for his return.

"Once ten girls were waiting to join a wedding feast. They didn't know how long it would be before the bridegroom would turn up, and so they all brought lamps with them, but only five of the girls thought to bring some spare oil with them. The other five brought their lamps but didn't have any spare oil.

"Time passed, and the bridegroom didn't come. One by one, the girls fell asleep. Then suddenly, at midnight, a cry rang out, for the bridegroom was coming. The girls woke up and rushed to light their lamps, but those of the foolish girls began to flicker straight away, for their oil had run out."

"The foolish girls turned to the other girls and begged them to spare them some of their oil, but the wise girls replied sadly, 'No, there isn't enough for all of us. You'll have to go and buy some more!' And the wise girls went off to join the bridegroom and went in with him to the feast.

"By the time the foolish girls returned with lighted lamps, the door was shut, and though they knocked loudly, they were told, 'You are too late. I don't know who you are!'"

Jesus told his disciples, "Always be ready, because you don't know the day or the hour of my return!"

What must we do to be prepared? Invite Jesus to come into our hearts!

The Great Banquet

"Once," said Jesus, "there was a king who was planning on holding a great feast to celebrate his son's wedding. He spent days planning it and inviting all the people that he wanted to share the occasion with.

"At last, it was ready. The king sent servants to tell the guests that it was time to come. Yet every last one of them had some or other excuse—they were busy with work, they had to feed the animals, their wife was sick . . . Not one of them bothered to stop what they were doing and come to the feast—and some were even rude and nasty to the servants!

"When the king heard this, he was furious. 'They don't deserve to come!' he told his servants in disgust. 'Go back outside, and this time go and invite all the poor people, anyone who is blind or crippled or lame and bring them in to enjoy the banquet!'

"And when this had been done, and there were still some empty places at the table, the king told his servants to search even farther afield and find yet more people, and make them come in so that his house would be full. As for the original, ungrateful guests who couldn't be bothered to turn up, the king vowed that not a single one of them would get even a taste of his feast!

"And what a wonderful feast it was! The tables were creaking under the weight of all delicious things to eat. Everyone had a lovely time!"

God had invited his people to be saved through his Son, Jesus Christ, but many had refused to accept Jesus as their Saviour—they made all kind of excuses to explain why he wasn't the Son of God, and took refuge in all their laws and traditions. So God extended his invitation all across the world—to everybody, not just the Jews.

God has invited us all to his wonderful feast—let's not miss out!

Lost and Found

The Pharisees and teachers of the law got upset when Jesus hung out with the "wrong sort" of people. They muttered amongst themselves when they saw Jesus mixing with tax collectors and people who had done bad things. They didn't understand what Jesus was trying to say about forgiveness. He tried to get them to see that there will be far more rejoicing in heaven over the one sinner who repents than over the ninety-nine good people who don't need to repent.

He said to them, "Imagine you had a hundred sheep and lost one of them. How would you feel? Wouldn't you leave the other ninety-nine safe and sound, and rush off to look for the lost one? Don't you think you would search high and low, in the wind or the rain or the snow, and keep on searching until you found it? And when you did find it, don't you think you would be so thrilled that you would rush home and celebrate?"

"Or picture a woman," continued Jesus, "who had ten silver coins and who lost one of those precious coins. Wouldn't she light a lamp? Don't you think she would take a brush and sweep every single corner of the room, and search every nook and cranny until she found it? And when she did find it, how happy and relieved would she be? Don't you think she would get all her friends and neighbours together and tell them about the lost coin, and how she had found it, and ask them to be happy for her?"

God cares about each and every one of us. He loves all the people who believe in him and try to live in the way he teaches. But that isn't enough. No, we are all so important to him that he will try to save every last one of us.

The Prodigal Son

Jesus told another story to explain how God loves to forgive us and how happy he is when sinners admit they're wrong and return to him.

"Once there was a man who had two sons," began Jesus. "One day, the youngest son came to his father and asked him if he could have the money that he would inherit after his father died. He wanted the money now because he longed to go travelling and exploring and do lots of fun things and be his own boss. He didn't want to stay at home on the farm. It was too boring!

"The father was sad, but he gave his son the money without any argument, and sent him on his way with a sigh.

"At first, the young man had a marvellous time. He went to some wonderful places, met some interesting people and basically did whatever he wanted, whenever he wanted. Life was fun!"

"But time went on," continued Jesus, "and the young man spent more and more of his money. Soon, it was all gone. Every last penny! Now he had no choice but to look for work, for he had no money for a place to stay or even for food. He ended up working for a pig farmer. All day long he looked after the pigs, cleaning out the pigsty, and giving them food. He was so hungry that he found himself wishing he could eat the scraps he was giving to the animals!

"At last he thought, 'This is ridiculous! My father feeds his servants better than this!' and he decided to go home and tell him how sorry he was and how silly he had been. 'I'm not worthy of being his son,' he thought to himself, 'but maybe he will let me work on the farm.'

"When his father saw him coming, he rushed to hug him. The young man tried to tell him that he was not fit to be called his son, but his father shushed him, and told his servants to bring his finest robe for his son and to kill the prize calf for a feast.

"Not everyone was quite so thrilled. The older son was angry that he had worked hard all this time, and nobody had ever held a feast for him! Yet here came his brother, having squandered all his money, and his father couldn't wait to throw a party!

"'My son,' the father said to him patiently, 'you are always with me, and all I have is yours. But celebrate with me now, for your brother was dead to me and is alive again; he was lost and is found!'"

Like the boy in the story, we don't always make the right choices. Sometimes we make mistakes and do silly things. But isn't it good to know that God is always ready and willing to forgive us, and to welcome us home with open arms?

The Rich Man and the Beggar

Once Jesus told a story about two very different men who led very different lives. "There was once a rich man," began Jesus, "who lived a life of luxury. He lived in a grand house, and wore fine clothes, and had lots of servants. Every day his dining table was covered with delicious plates of food. Every day was a feast!

"Now, just outside his house you would find a poor, hungry beggar named Lazarus, whose skin was covered with sores. He sat on the roadside day after day, hoping desperately for a scrap of food or a coin. Lazarus had nowhere to live, and hardly anything to eat. As he sat outside the rich man's house, enticing smells would waft past torment his empty stomach. How he longed for even the crumbs which fell from the rich man's table! How happy he would have been with just their leftovers. But the rich man never stopped to think about poor Lazarus. In fact, he'd been sitting outside his gate for so long that he hardly even noticed him anymore.

"At last Lazarus' suffering was over, for he died and the angels carried him up to heaven to Abraham, where he felt no more pain or cold or hunger.

"Some time after, the rich man also died, but when he passed away no angels came for him. Instead, he was sent to the place for wicked people, for he had been mean and selfish. In torment, he looked up to heaven and begged, 'Father Abraham, please take pity on me and send Lazarus to dip his finger in water and cool my tongue, for I'm so thirsty!'

"But Abraham replied, 'Did you take pity on Lazarus? Did you give him food when he was hungry? You had a great time on earth, while Lazarus was suffering, but now he is looked after up here, and it is your turn to suffer.'

"'Then please, Father Abraham,' pleaded the rich man, 'at least warn my brothers before it is too late, so that they don't make the same mistakes that I did!'

"'Oh, son,' said Abraham, shaking his head sadly, 'they already have the writings of Moses and the prophets to warn them. It's their own fault if they don't change their ways in time!'"

Things don't always work out for us in life, but if we let God into our hearts and into our lives, he will make things right for us in heaven. And if we are given gifts in this lifetime, let's use them unselfishly to help other people who aren't as well off as we are.

Bags of Gold

Jesus told his followers a story about a man who was heading off on a long journey. He left his money with his servants so that they could make use of it. He gave one of them five bags of gold, another two bags, and one bag to the third, according to their abilities.

Some time later he returned. He was delighted when the first two servants told him they had doubled the bags they had been given. He knew he could trust them, and put them in charge of many things.

But when the third servant told him he had hidden the gold as he had been scared to lose it, the man was angry. "You have been wicked and lazy," he exclaimed, and he gave the bag of gold to the first servant and had the lazy one thrown out!

God expects us to use whatever gifts he has given us. If we do, he will give us even more, but if we don't, he may take them away and give them to someone who *will* use them!

The Last Will Be First

Jesus told a parable: "The kingdom of heaven is like the vineyard owner who needed lots of work done, so he went out early one morning to the marketplace to hire some workers. There were plenty of men hanging around, so the vineyard owner offered them a certain amount of money for the day and set them to work.

"Later that day, he went back to the marketplace, hired more men, and told them he'd pay them whatever was right. He did the same at lunchtime and in the afternoon. When he went back to the marketplace at about five o'clock, there were still some men hanging around, and he asked why they were wasting their time. 'No one offered us any work,' the men said, which was a bit silly, since the owner had been there several times! Still, he told them that they could come and work for him.

"The vineyard bustled with activity, and lots of work was done that day. When evening came, the owner called his foreman to him and told him to pay the workers, beginning with the last ones hired.

"The workers who were hired late received the same amount that had been promised to the first workers. So when those at the back of the queue, the ones who had been hired first, came to receive their pay, they expected to get more because they had worked longer, but they were given exactly the same amount as the others.

"At this, they began to grumble. 'They only worked for one hour,' complained one, 'but you've given them the same as those of us who worked all day long in the blazing heat! How is that fair?'

"The owner answered, 'I'm not being unfair. Didn't you agree to work for this amount? I paid you what we agreed. I want to give the one hired last the same as you. Don't I have the right to do what I want with my own money? Or are you annoyed I'm being generous?'

"So the last will be first, and the first will be last."

Some people will serve God all their life, and their reward will be everlasting life in heaven. Other will do bad things and won't listen to God until the very end of their life, when they feel truly sorry and let him into their heart. God will reward them with everlasting life in heaven, too! Everyone who believes in God and opens their heart to him will receive the same reward—not because God is being unfair to those who have believed in him all along, but because he's being generous to *all* of us!

The Wicked Tenants

Jesus knew that the priests and the Pharisees often obeyed the letter of the law but didn't understand the real meaning of the law—they said the right things, without really letting God into their hearts.

He told them a story. "There was once a man who had two sons. He said to the older one, 'Son, go and work in the vineyard today.'

"'I don't want to,' grumbled the son, but later reluctantly he went.

"The father went to his other son and asked the same thing.

"'Sure,' answered the son straight away, but he didn't actually go."

Jesus looked around, "Which son actually did what his father wanted?"

"The older one," they answered.

You see, what we *do* is more important than what we *say* we will do!

Jesus told another story . . .

"There was once a man who planted some grapes, rented the vineyard to some farmers and then went away. At harvest time he sent a servant to collect his share of the fruit. But instead of giving him what they owed him, the wicked tenants beat the servant and sent him away with nothing!

"The man couldn't believe what had happened, so he sent another servant, but again they beat him and sent him away empty-handed. He sent a third, and that one was killed!

"In the end, the owner decided to send his own beloved son. 'Surely they will respect him,' he said to himself.

"But when the tenants saw him coming, they plotted amongst themselves. 'This is the owner's son,' they said. 'If we get rid of him then we will become the new owners!' And they threw him out of the vineyard and killed him."

Jesus looked at the priests and Pharisees. "What do you think the owner of the vineyard will do to the tenants when he finds out?"

"He'll kill them and give the vineyard to others who will treat him fairly," they replied. But when they realised that Jesus had really been talking about them, they felt tricked and angry!

You see, God sent many special people, such as Moses and David and Isaiah, to tell people how much he loved them, and to warn them to mend their ways. But the people didn't want to listen, and so, at last, he sent his own Son, Jesus . . .

God has given us so many chances. Let's not miss this one!